The
DRAGON
ORACLE

Summon the energy of the mysterious East
to fulfill your dreams, desires, and destiny

Gillian Stokes

BARNES & NOBLE

NEW YORK

This 2006 edition published by
Barnes and Noble Publishing, Inc.
by arrangement with Quantum Publishing

Illustrator: Ch'en-Ling

2006 Barnes & Noble Publishing

ISBN-13: 978-0-7607-8220-0
ISBN-10: 0-7607-8220-2

Printed in China

1 3 5 7 9 10 8 6 4 2

Contents

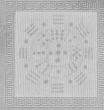

Introduction

This book offers a fascinating introduction to the cultural beliefs and methods of divination used for centuries in China and the Far East. Central to them all is the belief in a fundamental life energy called chi, from which all things are formed and which flows constantly through us and around us.

◄ A family setting off firecrackers in celebration of the Chinese New Year.

The aim of Chinese astrological systems is to discover how chi energy affects us and our surroundings at any particular time, so that we can strive to achieve harmony and balance in our lives. Understanding the flow of chi not only forms the basis for oracular systems, but also underlies practices such as acupuncture and tai chi. Chinese astrological methods are complex, so this book begins by examining the Eastern worldview: the basic concept of chi, how it manifests

▲ Living in harmony with your environment lies at the heart of all Eastern wisdom and divination methods.

itself in the opposite but complementary aspects of yin and yang, and how yin and yang sustain the five elements of the physical world from which all things are created. Having a basic knowledge of Chinese calendar systems is also important. Did you know, for example, that the Chinese have both a solar and a lunar calendar, and that the Chinese "hour" is 120 minutes long?

This book gives a simplified but clear explanation of these basic concepts, then provides an informative introduction to twelve-animal astrology, the I Ching, magic square astrology, and feng shui. These ancient arts can help us to understand the forces that have affected our lives in the past, to perceive the influences that are currently acting upon us, and to work in a positive way with the patterns of energy that will arise in the future. So delve into the oracles of the ancient East and bring your dragon out to play.

◄ Promoting a healthy flow of chi through the body is the aim of Chinese healing systems such as tai chi and acupuncture.

The Chinese Dragon

Chinese dragons, called lung, were beloved mythical creatures in ancient folklore. Four of them represented the supernatural forces underlying the elements of fire, earth, spirit, and water. Chinese people sometimes describe themselves with pride as the descendants of the dragon.

Able to encompass the world with their wings, to draw the moon and the sun across the sky, and to creep into the tiniest crevice, dragons were called upon whenever water was needed. They were said to take many forms and possess the magical attributes of flying and shape-shifting. Associated with thunder, rivers, streams, and wells, these benevolent bringers of rain were kings and lords of the waters and were thought especially important because they controlled fertility.

▲ The dragons on this 18th-century Chinese vase are depicted pursuing sacred pearls of wisdom among the clouds.

◄ Dragons are frequently used to adorn special buildings in China, especially during celebrations.

Dragons became regarded as the guardians of China's ruling emperors. With their five-clawed feet and huge wings, they would fight mighty battles with the sun to bring life-giving rain to the emperor's people. These powerful creatures, each said to have a pearl of wisdom in its mouth, symbolize the yang principle in Taoism, and their benevolent presence attracts the yin principles of clouds and water according to the laws of change—yin interchanging with yang in a never-ending cycle—that govern the universe.

The dragon is also the fifth of the twelve animals of Chinese astrology, in which role it is guardian of the east and sunrise, and symbolizes spring rains.

▶ A dragon embroidered on pink silk. Only the emperor and his family were allowed to wear garments decorated with the imperial five-clawed dragon.

Dragons are associated with water, and have been called upon since ancient times to bring rain and fertility to the land.

The EASTERN WORLDVIEW

Eastern wisdom and divination methods all draw on a common worldview, or cosmology. All creation is said to flow from one limitless force, known as chi. The constant movement of chi through, within, and around all things causes changes that manifest in the opposite energies of yin and yang. Yin and yang in turn sustain the core energy of the five physical elements, from which all things are created. Interpreting the interactions of yin and yang and the five elements forms the root of all Chinese divination systems.

▲ The bagua on this Chinese altar symbolizes the different manifestations of chi and how they interact.

Chi

It is Chinese philosophy that "all is one"—a boundless and ever-changing energy called chi. Chi is limitless potential from which all things take form and to which all things return once material decays to the point that it can no longer contain the chi energy. Chi flows through and around everything, and all is in a state of constant motion. In China it is believed that after the death of the body, the life spirit returns to this limitless state. Freed from the constraints of form as a point of reference, time has no meaning but existence continues. It is quite normal for Chinese people to continue to involve dead relatives dwelling in the spirit realm in daily life by means of rites and rituals.

Traveling Among Streams and Mountains by Fan Kuan. The interplay of yin (streams) and yang (mountains) is a common subject in Chinese art.

▲ Plants
(yin) and people
(yang) form just one of the
many yin/yang dualities that exist.

Yin and Yang

Change and oneness are at the root of Chinese belief. Yin and yang are complementary but opposite aspects of the one energy, chi. Whatever form the chi energy is expressing now is inevitably going to reach a limit from which it will fall into its opposite form of expression, only to repeat the cycle again and again, constantly changing from yin to yang and back again in a never-ending cycle. The interaction of yin and yang principles is traditionally depicted as an interlocked circle divided equally into white and black halves, each bearing the seed of its opposite in the form of a dot of the opposing color.

As well as interacting with each other, yin and yang are interdependent. In other words, night needs day if it is to have meaning, and so with every other duality imaginable: active/passive, winter/summer, spring growth/fall decay, heat/cold, up/down, and so on. It is by knowing what a thing is not, that we know what it is. Dynamic interaction between these opposing forces produces change. You will probably find that you recognize both aspects within yourself. This is because we contain both energies to a different and fluctuating degree. However, we all have a dominant aspect. Look on the lunar calendar chart on pages 17–19 to discover whether yin or yang governed your year of birth; this is your dominant aspect.

YIN/YANG DUALITIES

Yin	Yang
Feminine	Masculine
Passive	Active
Negative	Positive
Dark	Light
Soft	Hard
Receptive	Penetrating
Earth	Heaven
Valleys	Mountains
Moon	Sun
Water	Fire
Clouds	Sunshine
Plants	People
Inanimate objects	Animals
Even numbers	Odd numbers

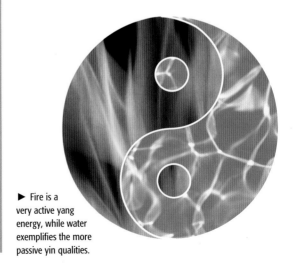

▶ Fire is a
very active yang
energy, while water
exemplifies the more
passive yin qualities.

The Five Elements

Five invisible energies (wu hsing, or five movers) are said to influence the physical forms we know as fire, earth, metal, water, and wood. Each of these five elements is associated with specific qualities and the changing cycles of the seasons. (The Western element air is not an Oriental element since it is ever-present in the form of chi, the breath of life that permeates all.) We all possess the qualities of the five elements in a unique combination, and the degree to which any element predominates determines the degree of balance in that area of our lives. Some elements are complementary, while others conflict. Look on the lunar calendar chart on pages 17–19 to discover the element that governed your year of birth; this is your dominant element.

▶ There are four elements in the West (fire, earth, water, and air) but in the East there are five (fire, earth, water, metal, and wood). The Western element air is not an Oriental element because it represents chi, the breath of life that is ever-present in the world.

THE FIVE ELEMENTS AND THEIR ASSOCIATIONS

Fire	Earth	Metal	Water	Wood
South	Center	West	North	East
Early summer	Late summer	Fall	Winter	Spring
Morning	Afternoon	Evening	Night	Sunrise
Red	Yellow	White	Black	Green
Expansion	Stability	Maturity	Renewal	Growth
Inspirational	Practical	Managerial	Intellectual	Analytical

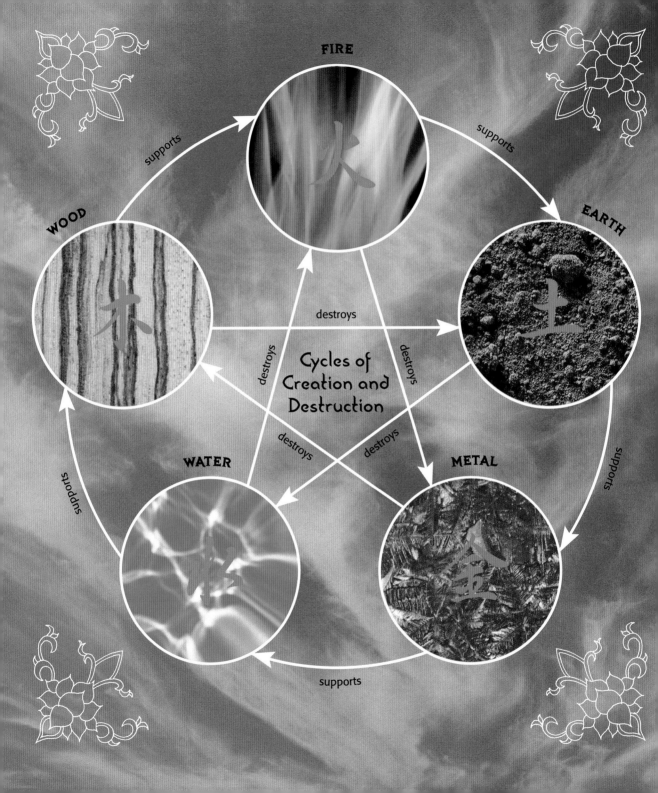

FIRE

WOOD

EARTH

WATER

METAL

supports

supports

supports

supports

supports

destroys

destroys

destroys

destroys

destroys

Cycles of
Creation and
Destruction

CYCLES OF CREATION AND DESTRUCTION

- **Fire** is supported by wood, beneficial to earth, melts metal, and is doused by water.
- **Earth** is enriched by fire, beneficial to metal, exhausts water, and is plundered by wood.
- **Metal** is assisted by earth, enables water, obstructs wood, and is checked by fire.
- **Water** is enabled by metal, feeds wood, douses fire, and is blocked by earth.
- **Wood** is fed by water, feeds fire, depletes earth, and is diminished by metal.

▲ The mountains (yang) and water (yin) in this landscape are in perfect balance.

▼ Try to achieve balance in all areas of your life, expending as much energy on family activities as you do in the work place.

Creating Balance

Balancing the flow of chi is central to Chinese philosophy. You can therefore use yin and yang and the five elements to recognize your own characteristics, identify prevailing conditions in your life, change predicted futures, and restore harmony. This could involve changing job or where you live, or less dramatically, what color you wear and the position of your furniture according to feng shui principles (see pages 50–61).

To counter negative aspects in your life, for example, introduce the element that will absorb or check them. For instance, in a strongly yang environment, such as a building situated amid flat, open space in full sunlight, increase yin by planting shrubs and trees to create shade, balance, and harmony. Similarly, if you have to face a hostile, fiery competitor at work, arrange the location of your next meeting so that it is influenced by water (a north-facing room, perhaps), to douse fiery passions or at least reduce them to steam.

If one part of your life seems to be going extremely well, you should always consider whether it is leading to imbalance and disharmony in other areas of your life and take action accordingly. For instance, too much inner creativity may exact a price on physical health. Remember, a life lived in balance is the way of the East.

The CHINESE YEAR

▼ A Tibetan calendar featuring the lo shu magic square, eight trigrams, and 12 astrological animals.

There are many different Chinese calendar cycles, which together provide a complex means of recording an extremely precise set of influences that can affect your life. In common with all astrological belief systems, Chinese astrologers assert that the moment you are born the alignment of the planets radiates a specific energy pattern that you absorb. If you were born a moment later, the energy pattern would have been different, because the planets would have moved. In China it is believed that these energetic influences follow a 60-year cycle, originally noted and classified as long ago as 2637 B.C. for Emperor Huang Ti.

▲ A Chinese emperor and his family. The imperial court devised and issued a detailed calendar each year.

The Solar Calendar

The Chinese solar calendar was devised as an agricultural tool and is the most regular of the Chinese calendar cycles. Scholars working for the emperor named each of the 24 fortnights of the year after the type of weather generally observed to occur in China's prime agricultural region during that time. Farmers learned exactly when to expect floods, when to plant, when to harvest, when pests would be likely to attack crops, and so on. The solar calendar runs concurrently with the lunar calendar (see page 16), and they coincide once every 19 years.

THE SOLAR CALENDAR

Sovereign Hexagram	Aspect	Names of Fortnights	Commencing	Sovereign Hexagram	Aspect	Names of Fortnights	Commencing
T'ai	Yang	Beginning of spring	Feb 5	P'i	Yin	Beginning of fall	Aug 8
		The rains	Feb 20			End of heat	Aug 24
Ta chuang	Yang	Awakening of creatures	Mar 7	Kuan	Yin	White dews	Sep 8
		Spring equinox	Mar 22			Fall equinox	Sep 24
Kuai	Yang	Clear and bright	Apr 6	Po	Yin	Cold dews	Oct 9
		Rain showers	Apr 21			Descent of hoar frost	Oct 24
Ch'ien	Yang	Beginning of summer	May 6	K'un	Yin	Beginning of winter	Nov 8
		Lesser fullness	May 22			Lesser snow	Nov 23
Kou	Yang	Grain in ear	Jun 7	Fu	Yin	Greater snow	Dec 7
		Summer solstice	Jun 22			Winter solstice	Dec 22
Tun	Yang	Lesser heat	Jul 8	Lin	Yin	Lesser cold	Jan 6
		Greater heat	Jul 24			Greater cold	Jan 21

The Lunar Calendar

The lunar calendar measures months and years according to the moon's cycle, and the phases of the moon govern the timing of public festivals and private events. For example, the date of the Chinese New Year occurs at the second new moon after the winter solstice, and can therefore be anywhere between late January and late February. A lunar year is composed of either 12 or 13 months (when necessary, an extra month is added to make sure that the winter solstice—December 22—occurs in month 11).

One of 12 animals is assumed to influence each lunar year. The animal cycle repeats every 12 years in the same order: Rat, Ox, Tiger, Rabbit, Dragon, Snake, Horse, Goat, Monkey, Rooster, Dog, and finally, Pig. Each Chinese year is therefore identified as the Year of the Dragon, the Year of the Snake, and so on. Each year is also believed to be dominated by either yin or yang energy and by one of the five elements; these, too, repeat in cycles each year. A complete cycle of animals, elements, and yin and yang takes 60 years.

▲ The Chinese New Year is determined by the lunar calendar, and is celebrated throughout the world with splendid dragon dances.

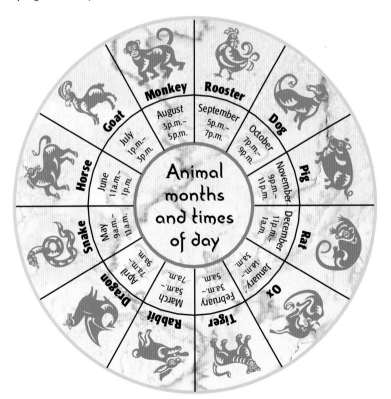

Animal Months and Times of Day

In addition to dominating a particular year, the 12 animals are associated with the months of the year and with 12 times of day. These 12 times of day are called "hours," although each covers a two-hour period. Your year, month, and time of birth together form the basis for divining when you will be more or less susceptible to positive and negative energies in your daily life. It is also believed that year animals represent your outer personality, month animals indicate how you will behave in relationships, and that hour animals reflect your true, inner nature.

Note: It is not possible to print the lunar month cycle for every year in a book of this size, so approximate Western months have been indicated for each of the 12 animals.

The Chinese Almanac

Each year the emperor published detailed calendar forecasts in the form of the Chinese almanac (the *T'ung Shu*, or *Know Everything Book*). Propitious times for getting married, moving house, or burying deceased relatives are among the numerous forecasts to be found in the almanac. The compass directions of favorable and unfavorable planetary energies enable detailed personal activities to be planned in association with the calendar and one's personal horoscope for maximum success. The almanac helped to reinforce the emperor's power, since he alone issued it. Recent Chinese political history led to the almanac being suppressed in its country of origin, but it remains popular among its people living elsewhere.

▼ A page from a modern Chinese almanac featuring a feng shui chart.

THE LUNAR CALENDAR

Year	Begins	Ends	Aspect	Element	Animal
1900	Jan 31, 1900	Feb 18, 1901	Yang	Metal	Rat
1901	Feb 19, 1901	Feb 7, 1902	Yin	Metal	Ox
1902	Feb 8, 1902	Jan 28, 1903	Yang	Water	Tiger
1903	Jan 29, 1903	Feb 15, 1904	Yin	Water	Rabbit
1904	Feb 16, 1904	Feb 3, 1905	Yang	Wood	Dragon
1905	Feb 4, 1905	Jan 24, 1906	Yin	Wood	Snake
1906	Jan 25, 1906	Feb 12, 1907	Yang	Fire	Horse
1907	Feb 13, 1907	Feb 1, 1908	Yin	Fire	Goat
1908	Feb 2, 1908	Jan 21, 1909	Yang	Earth	Monkey
1909	Jan 22, 1909	Feb 9, 1910	Yin	Earth	Rooster
1910	Feb 10, 1910	Jan 29, 1911	Yang	Metal	Dog
1911	Jan 30, 1911	Feb 17, 1912	Yin	Metal	Pig
1912	Feb 18, 1912	Feb 5, 1913	Yang	Water	Rat
1913	Feb 6, 1913	Jan 25, 1914	Yin	Water	Ox
1914	Jan 26, 1914	Feb 13, 1915	Yang	Wood	Tiger
1915	Feb 14, 1915	Feb 2, 1916	Yin	Wood	Rabbit
1916	Feb 3, 1916	Jan 22, 1917	Yang	Fire	Dragon
1917	Jan 23, 1917	Feb 10, 1918	Yin	Fire	Snake
1918	Feb 11, 1918	Jan 31, 1919	Yang	Earth	Horse
1919	Feb 1, 1919	Feb 19, 1920	Yin	Earth	Goat
1920	Feb 20, 1920	Feb 7, 1921	Yang	Metal	Monkey
1921	Feb 8, 1921	Jan 27, 1922	Yin	Metal	Rooster
1922	Jan 28, 1922	Feb 15, 1923	Yang	Water	Dog
1923	Feb 16, 1923	Feb 4, 1924	Yin	Water	Pig
1924	Feb 5, 1924	Jan 24, 1925	Yang	Wood	Rat
1925	Jan 25, 1925	Feb 12, 1926	Yin	Wood	Ox
1926	Feb 13, 1926	Feb 1, 1927	Yang	Fire	Tiger
1927	Feb 2, 1927	Jan 22, 1928	Yin	Fire	Rabbit
1928	Jan 23, 1928	Feb 9, 1929	Yang	Earth	Dragon
1929	Feb 10, 1929	Jan 29, 1930	Yin	Earth	Snake
1930	Jan 30, 1930	Feb 16, 1931	Yang	Metal	Horse
1931	Feb 17, 1931	Feb 5, 1932	Yin	Metal	Goat
1932	Feb 6, 1932	Jan 25, 1933	Yang	Water	Monkey
1933	Jan 26, 1933	Feb 13, 1934	Yin	Water	Rooster

1934	Feb 14, 1934	Feb 3, 1935	Yang	Wood	Dog
1935	Feb 4, 1935	Jan 23, 1936	Yin	Wood	Pig
1936	Jan 24, 1936	Feb 10, 1937	Yang	Fire	Rat
1937	Feb 11, 1937	Jan 30, 1938	Yin	Fire	Ox
1938	Jan 31, 1938	Feb 18, 1939	Yang	Earth	Tiger
1939	Feb 19, 1939	Feb 7, 1940	Yin	Earth	Rabbit
1940	Feb 8, 1940	Jan 26, 1941	Yang	Metal	Dragon
1941	Jan 27, 1941	Feb 14, 1942	Yin	Metal	Snake
1942	Feb 15, 1942	Feb 4, 1943	Yang	Water	Horse
1943	Feb 5, 1943	Jan 24, 1944	Yin	Water	Goat
1944	Jan 25, 1944	Feb 12, 1945	Yang	Wood	Monkey
1945	Feb 13, 1945	Feb 1, 1946	Yin	Wood	Rooster
1946	Feb 2, 1946	Jan 21, 1947	Yang	Fire	Dog
1947	Jan 22, 1947	Feb 9, 1948	Yin	Fire	Pig
1948	Feb 10, 1948	Jan 28, 1949	Yang	Earth	Rat
1949	Jan 29, 1949	Feb 16, 1950	Yin	Earth	Ox
1950	Feb 17, 1950	Feb 5, 1951	Yang	Metal	Tiger
1951	Feb 6, 1951	Jan 26, 1952	Yin	Metal	Rabbit
1952	Jan 27, 1952	Feb 13, 1953	Yang	Water	Dragon
1953	Feb 14, 1953	Feb 2, 1954	Yin	Water	Snake
1954	Feb 3, 1954	Jan 23, 1955	Yang	Wood	Horse
1955	Jan 24, 1955	Feb 11, 1956	Yin	Wood	Goat
1956	Feb 12, 1956	Jan 30, 1957	Yang	Fire	Monkey
1957	Jan 31, 1957	Feb 17, 1958	Yin	Fire	Rooster
1958	Feb 18, 1958	Feb 7, 1959	Yang	Earth	Dog
1959	Feb 8, 1959	Jan 27, 1960	Yin	Earth	Pig
1960	Jan 28, 1960	Feb 14, 1961	Yang	Metal	Rat
1961	Feb 15, 1961	Feb 4, 1962	Yin	Metal	Ox
1962	Feb 5, 1962	Jan 24, 1963	Yang	Water	Tiger
1963	Jan 25, 1963	Feb 12, 1964	Yin	Water	Rabbit
1964	Feb 13, 1964	Feb 1, 1965	Yang	Wood	Dragon
1965	Feb 2, 1965	Jan 20, 1966	Yin	Wood	Snake
1966	Jan 21, 1966	Feb 8, 1967	Yang	Fire	Horse
1967	Feb 9, 1967	Jan 29, 1968	Yin	Fire	Goat
1968	Jan 30, 1968	Feb 16, 1969	Yang	Earth	Monkey
1969	Feb 17, 1969	Feb 5, 1970	Yin	Earth	Rooster
1970	Feb 6, 1970	Jan 26, 1971	Yang	Metal	Dog

1971	Jan 27, 1971	Jan 15, 1972	Yin	Metal	Pig
1972	Jan 16, 1972	Feb 2, 1973	Yang	Water	Rat
1973	Feb 3, 1973	Jan 22, 1974	Yin	Water	Ox
1974	Jan 23, 1974	Feb 10, 1975	Yang	Wood	Tiger
1975	Feb 11, 1975	Jan 30, 1976	Yin	Wood	Rabbit
1976	Jan 31, 1976	Feb 17, 1977	Yang	Fire	Dragon
1977	Feb 18, 1977	Feb 6, 1978	Yin	Fire	Snake
1978	Feb 7, 1978	Jan 27, 1979	Yang	Earth	Horse
1979	Jan 28, 1979	Feb 15, 1980	Yin	Earth	Goat
1980	Feb 16, 1980	Feb 4, 1981	Yang	Metal	Monkey
1981	Feb 5, 1981	Jan 24, 1982	Yin	Metal	Rooster
1982	Jan 25, 1982	Feb 12, 1983	Yang	Water	Dog
1983	Feb 13, 1983	Feb 1, 1984	Yin	Water	Pig
1984	Feb 2, 1984	Feb 19, 1985	Yang	Wood	Rat
1985	Feb 20, 1985	Feb 8, 1986	Yin	Wood	Ox
1986	Feb 9, 1986	Jan 28, 1987	Yang	Fire	Tiger
1987	Jan 29, 1987	Feb 16, 1988	Yin	Fire	Rabbit
1988	Feb 17, 1988	Feb 5, 1989	Yang	Earth	Dragon
1989	Feb 6, 1989	Jan 26, 1990	Yin	Earth	Snake
1990	Jan 27, 1990	Feb 14, 1991	Yang	Metal	Horse
1991	Feb 15, 1991	Feb 3, 1992	Yin	Metal	Goat
1992	Feb 4, 1992	Jan 22, 1993	Yang	Water	Monkey
1993	Jan 23, 1993	Feb 9, 1994	Yin	Water	Rooster
1994	Feb 10, 1994	Jan 30, 1995	Yang	Wood	Dog
1995	Jan 31, 1995	Feb 18, 1996	Yin	Wood	Pig
1996	Feb 19, 1996	Feb 7, 1997	Yang	Fire	Rat
1997	Feb 8, 1997	Jan 27, 1998	Yin	Fire	Ox
1998	Jan 28, 1998	Feb 15, 1999	Yang	Earth	Tiger
1999	Feb 16, 1999	Feb 4, 2000	Yin	Earth	Rabbit
2000	Feb 5, 2000	Jan 23, 2001	Yang	Metal	Dragon
2001	Jan 24, 2001	Feb 11, 2002	Yin	Metal	Snake
2002	Feb 12, 2002	Jan 31, 2003	Yang	Water	Horse
2003	Feb 1, 2003	Jan 21, 2004	Yin	Water	Goat
2004	Jan 22, 2004	Feb 8, 2005	Yang	Wood	Monkey
2005	Feb 9, 2005	Jan 28, 2006	Yin	Wood	Rooster
2006	Jan 29, 2006	Feb 17, 2007	Yang	Fire	Dog
2007	Feb 18, 2007	Feb 6, 2008	Yin	Fire	Pig

Twelve-animal Astrology

Each Chinese year is named for one of 12 animals in a precise sequence maintained since ancient times. Other Eastern countries use alternatives to some of the Chinese animals—the Boar for the Pig; the Sheep for the Goat; the Buffalo for the Ox; the Cat or Hare for the Rabbit; and the Cockerel for the Rooster—but the symbolism remains the same. The characteristics assigned to each animal offer a light-hearted and broad insight into the character of those people born in that animal's year, but always remember that free will and personal choices can counteract these predictions.

Finding Your Astrological Animal

In the Western calendar New Year always falls on January 1, and is determined by the earth's position relative to the sun. However, the Chinese New Year is calculated according to the moon's cycle, and therefore occurs on a different calendar date each year. Refer to the lunar calendar chart on pages 17–19 to find out your Chinese astrological animal, then read about its characteristics on pages 22–23.

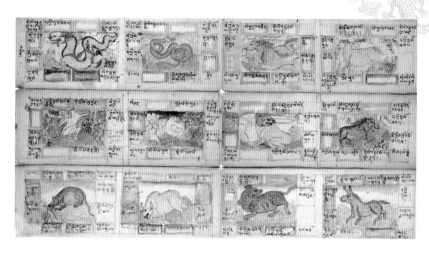

▲ Late 18th-century Tibetan manuscript featuring the 12 animals of Chinese astrology.

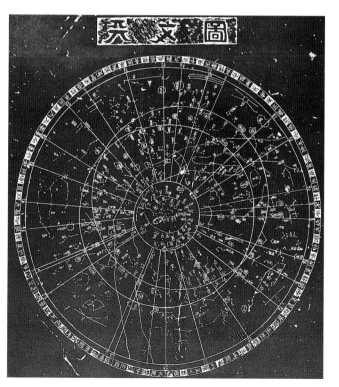

You may also wish to discover the animal that governs the month and time of your birth (see page 16). While your year animal represents your outer personality, the animal that dominates the month of your birth indicates how you behave in relationships, and the animal governing the time of your birth reveals your true, inner nature. Each animal is also associated with a particular element and yin or yang aspect (see pages 22–23), which represents its true nature, though the element and aspect that governed your year of birth is usually more dominant.

◄ An ancient Chinese planisphere, or star map, incorporating 1,400 stars and based on the 13th-century Suzhou planisphere. Animal astrology is linked with the lunar calendar, and requires complex astronomical calculations.

Animal Characteristics

Rat (yang, water)

Happy-go-lucky, cheerful, popular, and hard-working. Rat is smart and quick-witted, and hides any deeper feelings. A hoarder, Rat spends only if it is an investment that will pay dividends. Ambitious, practical, and clear-sighted, Rat usually succeeds. Bored by routine and timekeeping, Rat works best as an innovator.

Ox (yin, water)

Hard-working and resolute, Ox is loyal, dutiful, and true, but can find relationships a problem. A great traditionalist, particularly at home, Ox distrusts change and can be a bit of a moaner and become stuck in a rut. However, although steady and thoughtful, Ox is no fool.

Tiger (yang, wood)

Brave, forthright, and honorable. Keeps promises and expects others to do likewise. Confident and spontaneous to the point of recklessness, Tiger can seem arrogant to less dynamic folk. Life with a Tiger is never dull, but it can be risky. Tiger's recklessness can lead to failure, but a Tiger never stays down for long.

Rabbit (yin, wood)

Though quiet and sensitive, Rabbit loves company at home and at work. A natural diplomat who prefers to negotiate, not fight, Rabbit is fierce when cornered. Luckiest of the animals, Rabbit loves creature comforts and knows how to charm those who will supply them. Artistic, talented, considerate, and methodical, but sometimes fickle and devious.

Dragon (yang, wood)

Innovative, energetic, independent, and outgoing, the Dragon needs constant stimulation. Most loved, and hated, of the animals, Dragon has to be the center of attention. Generous and direct, Dragon can also be argumentative and demanding. Has a tendency to forget those less fortunate in the attempt to win at all costs.

Snake (yin, fire)

Wise, amusing, opportunistic, adaptable, and artistic, the Snake is a popular and powerful animal that wants only the best. Snake's speculative judgment is weak, but intuitive wisdom strong. In other words, Snakes are poor gamblers but good providers. Naturally secretive and somewhat jealous, infidelity is possible, but actually rare.

Horse (yang, fire)

Freedom-loving, industrious, and ambitious, if sometimes selfish, the Horse will roam far. Charming, unpredictable, and attractive, Horse makes a good entertainer. An amiable leader and good judge, Horse sometimes shows flashes of temper and can be too headstrong.

Goat (yin, fire)

Artistically creative, gentle, patient, quiet, and considerate, Goat is easily wounded by criticism. A lover of finery, Goat can be reckless and fickle, with a deep-seated hunger for luxury that can cause problems. Goat is not the ideal leader, but good manners and a loving nature compensate for any deficiencies in this popular animal.

Monkey (yang, metal)

Irreverent, ingenious, amusing, creative, and clever, the Monkey will do well in all areas of life. Although charming, generous, and considerate, Monkey can sometimes be impatient, selfish, and vain. Has a thriving imagination, lively humor, a natural inquisitiveness, a resourceful nature, and a deep-seated need to be surrounded by people.

Rooster (yin, metal)

Steady, punctual, reliable, enthusiastic, and hard-working, the Rooster is usually loyal to friends and family alike, but can be tactless and think it always knows best. Courageous and brave, Rooster is usually good with money, especially that of other people.

Dog (yang, metal)

Loyal, faithful, and brave, a follower not a leader. Usually modest, respectable, and restrained, a Dog can sometimes be impetuous. May suppress feelings and become prone to depression; Dogs set high standards for themselves and others. Dogs are always willing to help others and are generous to a fault.

Pig (yin, water)

A dependable and sociable team player, Pig makes a good leader or lover. Cultured and sensitive, Pig likes stability, leaving this animal vulnerable and insecure at times. Loves creature comforts and a cozy home. Pig's easy-going nature is often taken advantage of, but this animal can also display the aggression of a boar.

Animal Compatibility

Certain animals are deemed to be more compatible than others. If you place the 12 animals around a circle as though they were the hours on a clock face, and draw an equilateral triangle from the position of each sign, the animal signs that occupy the connecting triangle points are usually considered the most compatible, and those outside each triangle less so.

The sign directly opposite is generally thought to be the least compatible.

There are exceptions, however. Sometimes two very different animals can form the ideal partnership, because they each supply qualities absent in the other. For example, a reckless Tiger may be well matched by a more dependable Pig. On the other hand, although a Pig and a Rabbit should form an ideal match since they are both sensitive, in practice the Rabbit can be too fickle for the insecure Pig. The chart below therefore contains some exceptions to the clock-face theory.

Remember that any horoscope should take into account many more factors than merely the prevailing year and its animal, so if you have a wonderful relationship with an animal with whom you should be opposed, or a dreadful one with the animal you should be most compatible with, trust what you know. It is probable that other factors strongly outweigh those given here.

▲ A smart Rat and an outgoing Dragon make ideal business partners and lovers.

▼ The romantic Pig will shower the luxury-loving Goat with gifts of love.

ANIMAL COMPATIBILITY

Animal	Best	Good	Fair	Worst
Rat	Dragon	Monkey	Tiger, Dog	Horse, Snake, Goat
Ox	Snake, Rooster	Pig	Tiger, Dog, Ox	Goat, Monkey
Tiger	Dog, Horse	Dragon, Pig	Ox, Snake, Tiger	Monkey, Rabbit
Rabbit	Pig, Goat	Rabbit	Monkey, Horse, Dog	Rooster, Tiger
Dragon	Rat, Tiger, Snake, Monkey	Dragon, Rabbit	Horse, Goat	Dog
Snake	Snake, Ox, Rooster	Horse, Dragon	Tiger, Monkey	Pig
Horse	Dog, Tiger	Goat	Rabbit, Snake, Monkey, Pig, Ox	Rat
Goat	Pig, Rabbit	Horse	Dragon	Ox, Rooster, Monkey, Tiger. Rat
Monkey	Dragon, Pig, Monkey	Rat	Ox, Tiger, Rabbit	Horse, Dog
Rooster	Ox	Snake	Dragon, Horse, Monkey	Rabbit
Dog	Horse, Pig	Tiger	Rabbit	Dragon, Goat
Pig	Goat, Tiger	Dog, Pig	Rabbit	Horse, Snake

The Clock-face Theory
of Compatibility

The Chinese Tarot

You may use a set of cards depicting the 12 Chinese astrological animals to divine the answers to specific questions. If you do not have a set, you can easily make your own. You will need three sets of the 12 Chinese animals, 36 cards in all. By using three separate cards depicting each of the 12 animals, the influence of a particular animal may be revealed to be affecting your past, present, and future.

Asking a Question

If you have several alternative courses of action in mind, you should treat each question to a separate casting of the cards. Each question should refer to a specific issue—for example, "Will I succeed if I work with so-and-so?" Abstract or generalized questions of the "Will I be rich?" type cannot be answered by the cards because the outcomes depend on an infinite number of future decisions and influences.

Performing a Reading

There are many different tarot spreads that you can do; three are described here. Choose the spread that most appeals to you, or that seems most appropriate to the nature of your question. Hold the cards with their reverse side facing you and shuffle them, keeping your question in your mind while you do so. Cut the cards and reshuffle in this way three times. Now deal the cards in the pattern of the spread.

Bearing in mind the significance of each card's placement within a particular tarot spread, look up the animal characteristics on pages 22–23 to discover the answer to your question. Sometimes it may indicate that someone with those qualities has affected that area of your life, but more often it is simply the characteristics that each animal represents that are significant.

Remember that the answer that the cards provide could change in the light of future actions and influences. A tarot reading can only give an indication of the likely outcome; you are free to change your destiny.

THE CELESTIAL NINE-CARD SPREAD

This is the simplest spread to do, and involves laying out three sets of three cards, nine in all. Start with the bottom row and lay the cards from left to right.

1–3 The probable future outcome of your proposed action (1: immediate, 2: medium term, 3: distant future).

4–6 The present (take all three animal definitions into account when considering the meaning, as the present is an intermingling of these three qualities).

7–9 The past influences on your question (7: distant, 8: medium term, 9: immediate past).

THE EMPEROR'S EIGHT-CARD SPREAD

This spread is a little more complicated to interpret and involves laying eight cards, seven from right to left in a crescent shape above a single card that represents the question.

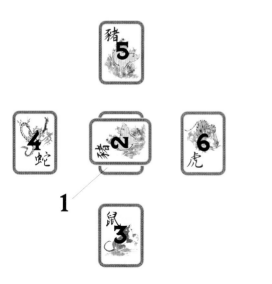

1 The question.
2 The past.
3 The present.
4 Hidden influences.
5 Difficulties to be faced.
6 The attitude of others.
7 The advisable manner to proceed.
8 The likely outcome.

THE HEAVENLY TEN-CARD SPREAD

This is the most complicated spread, but is useful when you require a detailed answer to your question and wish to understand more fully how the situation has arisen.

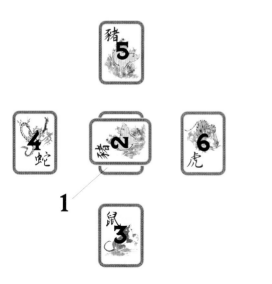

1 Your question, the present.
2 The immediate conflict, obstacles, or dilemma concerned with the question.
3 Past influences affecting the question or questioner.
4 The prevailing background situation.
5 The goal, the inner drive motivating the question.
6 The influences about to come into being in relation to the question.
7 Your present attitude.
8 What others think of your question, the influence of family, friends, colleagues, and so on.
9 The hopes and fears you have concerning the question.
10 The outcome, should you proceed in your potential endeavor as reflected by the influences at the moment of asking the question.

The I CHING

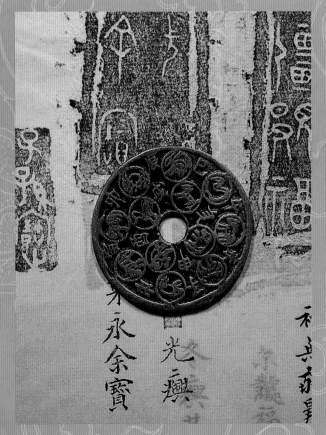

The I Ching, or Book of Changes, has been revered as a sacred book in China for at least 5,000 years. The book contains 64 interpretations that represent the changing balance of yin and yang energies. These interpretations can be consulted as a divinatory tool to provide answers to particular questions, or used for advice in their own right. Treat this oracle with the respect and reverence that is its due, and you will discover its accuracy for yourself.

Origins of the I Ching

The legendary first emperor of China, Fu Hsi, is said to have chosen a broken line to represent yin energy and a solid line to represent yang energy. He then combined pairs of yin and yang lines to create four offspring, representing greater yin and lesser yin, and greater yang and lesser yang. He then added an additional yin or yang line to each of these four pairs to create eight trigrams composed of three lines each. Each trigram was given a name and allocated various attributes (the trigrams and their attributes are used in feng shui; see pages 50–61).

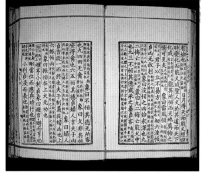

▲ Pages of the *I Ching*. The book has been a source of wisdom and divination for at least 5,000 years.

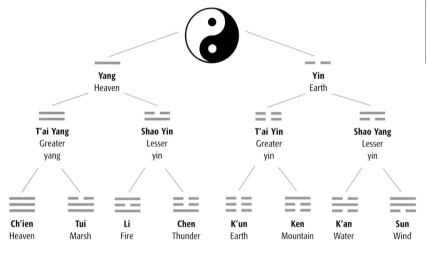

Yang Heaven	**Yin** Earth

T'ai Yang Greater yang	**Shao Yin** Lesser yin	**T'ai Yin** Greater yin	**Shao Yang** Lesser yin

Ch'ien Heaven	**Tui** Marsh	**Li** Fire	**Chen** Thunder	**K'un** Earth	**Ken** Mountain	**K'an** Water	**Sun** Wind

Around 2,000 years later, King Wen, the founder of the Chou dynasty, combined pairs of the trigrams to produce the 64 hexagrams of the I Ching that we know today. Several sages, including Confucius, contributed additional commentaries to the I Ching, though here we concentrate on the 64 main interpretations.

TRIGRAMS AND THEIR ASSOCIATIONS

Trigram	Name	Image	Attributes	Animal	Family Link	Direction
	Ch'ien	Heaven	Sky	Strength	Horse	Father	Northwest
	K'un	Earth	Fidelity	Submission	Ox	Mother	Southwest
	Chen	Thunder	Impulsiveness	Provocation	Dragon	Elder son	East
	K'an	Water	Danger	Flexibility	Pig	Middle son	North
	Ken	Mountain	Immobility	Inevitability	Dog	Younger son	Northeast
	Sun	Wind	Subtlety	Penetration	Fowl	Elder daughter	Southeast
	Li	Fire	Enlightenment	Warmth	Pheasant	Middle daughter	South
	Tui	Marsh	Joy	Magic	Goat	Younger daughter	West

◀ The original compass directions allocated to each trigram by Emperor Fu Hsi are known as the Former Heaven Sequence. King Wen later changed these to what is known as the Later Heaven Sequence (as shown here and in the feng shui chapter). While some feng shui practitioners prefer the original sequence, many only use it for locating gravesites and use the Later Heaven Sequence for homes of the living.

▲ Woodblock-printed copy of *The Book of Changes*, some yarrow sticks, and I Ching coins.

Consulting the I Ching

To consult the I Ching, you need to construct a hexagram while asking a specific question. Traditionally, a bundle of yarrow sticks was employed for creating hexagrams, but the simpler coin system described here is now widely used. The I Ching is believed to respond to the thoughts you hold while casting the coins or sticks.

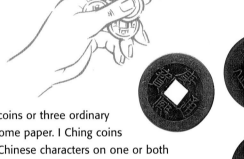

Yin side

Yang side

1. Asking a question

The question you ask should be important to you. Generalized or fanciful questions will fail, as will open-ended or abstract questions of the "Will I be rich?" variety. Since you retain the free will to change predicted outcomes, the oracle cannot generalize. Ask questions such as:

- *What should I do given such-and-such a situation?*
- *What will happen if I act in this way? (Create a hexagram while asking the question for each possible course of action.)*
- *What should I do to achieve a particular goal?*
- *Tell me more about a real person or event.*

2. Equipment

Find three I Ching coins or three ordinary coins, a pen, and some paper. I Ching coins are inscribed with Chinese characters on one or both sides. The most heavily inscribed side is known as the yang side and the less inscribed side is known as the yin side. If using ordinary coins, use heads as the yang side and tails as the yin side.

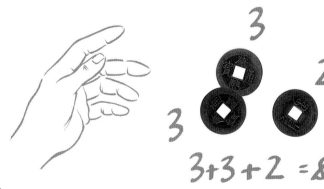

3. Tossing the coins

Throw the coins onto a level surface. Coins landing yang-side up have a value of 3; coins landing yin-side up have a value of 2. Add up the values of the three coins and write this figure down. The only score possible is 6, 7, 8, or 9.

4. Six numbers

Throw the coins five more times and write down the score each time to form a vertical column of six numbers, working from the bottom upward. The bottom number represents the score from the first throw, and the top number the score from the last throw.

5. Yin and yang lines

The score from each throw of the coins equates to a single line of the hexagram, which can be yin, yang, moving yin, or moving yang. Draw the appropriate line next to each of the six scores. Yin is traditionally shown as a broken line, as befits its passive and yielding nature. Yang is depicted as a solid line, in keeping with its firm and active principle. A moving yin line represents yin at the point where its energy is about to turn into its opposite state of yang; a moving yang line represents yang when it is about to turn into yin.

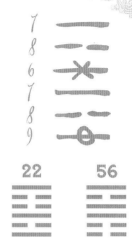

Score	Line	Description	Meaning
6		Broken line, becoming solid	Moving yin line
7		Solid line	Yang line
8		Broken line	Yin line
9		Solid line, becoming broken	Moving yang line

6. Hexagrams with no moving lines

If you have no moving lines, your hexagram is complete. Look at the hexagram finder chart on page 32 to figure out which number hexagram you have created. The example shown here is hexagram 52. Once you know the number of your hexagram, turn to the appropriate interpretation on pages 32–39 and read the answer to your question.

7. Hexagrams with moving lines

If you do have moving lines, you have the opportunity of obtaining two answers to your question, one for the immediate situation and another for the near future (when the energy represented by the moving lines will have changed). The easiest way to do this is to draw two hexagrams, one before the moving lines change and one after they have changed. For example, if your hexagram contains a moving yang line in the bottom position, draw the hexagram with a yang line at the bottom, then redraw it with a yin line at the bottom. The example shown here starts as hexagram 22 and becomes hexagram 56 when the moving lines have changed. Look at the hexagram finder chart on page 32 to figure out which number hexagrams you have created, then turn to the interpretations on pages 32–39.

HEXAGRAM FINDER

lower trigram \ upper trigram	☰	☳	☵	☶	☷	☴	☲	☱
☰	1	34	5	26	11	9	14	43
☳	25	51	3	27	24	42	21	17
☵	6	40	29	4	7	59	64	47
☶	33	62	39	52	15	53	56	31
☷	12	16	8	23	2	20	35	45
☴	44	32	48	18	46	57	50	28
☲	13	55	63	22	36	37	30	49
☱	10	54	60	41	19	61	38	58

Hexagram Interpretations

1 Yang

Creativity. You will achieve your goals through perseverance, but beware of complacency or recklessness.

2 Yin
Good fortune follows passive persistence. Exercise caution and modesty. Help may come from an unexpected quarter.

3 Growing Pains
Birth can be painful, whether of a child, a relationship, or a new venture. Suffer in silence; it will get better.

4 Youthful Folly
Repeated questions gain foolish answers. The inexperienced should learn from the wise.

5 Waiting
Delays likely. Be sincere and patient and all will be well. Exercise self-control until danger has passed.

6 Conflict
Caution. Some trouble is inevitable. Look before you leap or you could invite litigation.

7 The Army
Battle looms. Avoid reckless chances. With correct and diligent behavior, you can succeed.

8 Seeking Union
Intimacy. Relationships will go well if you give as well as take. Cooperation and sincerity are called for.

9 Minor Restraint
Obstacles are looming. With care, you can gain small victories. Make the best of the situation.

10 Treading
Difficult times can be overcome with patient humility and honest endeavor. Be polite but strong.

11 Peace
Good fortune. Be generous to others and you will benefit. What goes around, comes around.

12 Stagnation
Inauspicious. Little progress is possible. Plan for the future, but do not make moves yet.

13 Fellowship
Cooperation will bring success. Act now, remembering to think of others, and you will benefit.

14 Wealth
Wealth, progress, and good fortune. Help from authority. Avoid arrogance and be ready to learn.

15 Modesty
With humility, all will go well. Maintain your calm amid the storms. Be tolerant of others.

16 Enthusiasm
Confidence, clarity, and the support of others will win the day. Prepare your case well.

3

Growing Pains

This hexagram advises quiet patience when faced with difficulties related to growing up or embarking on new projects.

17 Following
Take a secondary position. Be flexible and follow the advice of others. Leadership is ill-advised.

18 Decay
Right former wrongs and success will follow. Repair what is decayed. Be scrupulously honest.

19 Conduct
Cooperate and fortune will be yours. Be generous and you will gain the support of others.

20 Contemplation
Self-knowledge will improve your luck. Consider well before taking action, but avoid hesitation.

21 Biting Through
Things do not go as planned. Firm personal action is needed to remove obstacles. Hesitate and you lose.

22 Beauty
The arts are favored. Restrict yourself to conventional actions and making small changes.

23 Collapse
Movement in any direction is ill-advised. Expect losses and begin planning for the future.

24 The Return
The tide is turning. Go with the flow and try something new. A time of rejuvenation.

25 The Innocent
Know your limitations and deepest desires. Wait for a better time and obstacles will pass.

26 Major Restraint
Setbacks are likely, but hard work can triumph. Great potential, but you must wait for your chance.

27 Nourishment
Avoid impetuous action. Exercise moderation in all things and you will be ready when the time comes.

28 Greatness Abounds
Know your strengths and weaknesses. Change is coming. Steady effort will now succeed.

29 The Deep
Danger threatens. Remain still and await help. Change will come, but wait for guidance.

30 Fire
Know your limitations and accept guidance. Reason and intellect will succeed if harnessed well.

31 Tension
Avoid envy. Cooperative ventures will do well, but do not compromise your principles.

32 Continuity
Perseverance and endurance will succeed. Avoid recklessness and listen to the advice of others.

33 Retreat
Take a step back and assess the situation. Trust your own judgment. Beware of tricksters.

34 Great Strength
Do as you would be done by and great fortune will follow. Be scrupulously fair and unselfish.

29

The Deep

This hexagram indicates that danger is on its way, and advises motionlessness until help arrives.

35 Progress

Great good fortune will come if you keep high ethical standards. Be honest in all your dealings.

36 Darkening of the Light

Hard times ahead. Be patient and they will pass. Maintain good grace while waiting for improvement.

37 The Family

Good fortune and happiness attends loyalty and consideration for others. Respect your loved ones.

38 Opposition

Sincere opposition. Avoid dogmatism and maintain flexibility. Find an honorable compromise.

39 Obstruction

Advance is futile, delay inevitable. Retreat and seek support. Treachery is possible.

40 Deliverance

A situation is coming to a head. Cut loose and move forward. Opportunity awaits firm action.

41 Decrease

Delays and disappointments. Cooperation will help. Avoid excess and share with others.

42 Increase

Opportunity knocks. Seize the day. Luck must change for the better, so make the most of it.

43 Breakthrough

Temporary prosperity, but losses imminent. Take precautions and plan ahead for future troubles.

44 Temptation

Beware of false advice and harm from others. Remain calm and trust your own judgment.

45 Assembling

Rich rewards are possible if you seek the help of others. Self-sufficiency is ill-advised.

46 Pushing Upward

Progress is steady. Avoid rash acts and cultivate superiors. Keep moving toward your goal.

44

Temptation

This hexagram warns against falling prey to false advice from others, no matter how appealing it may seem.

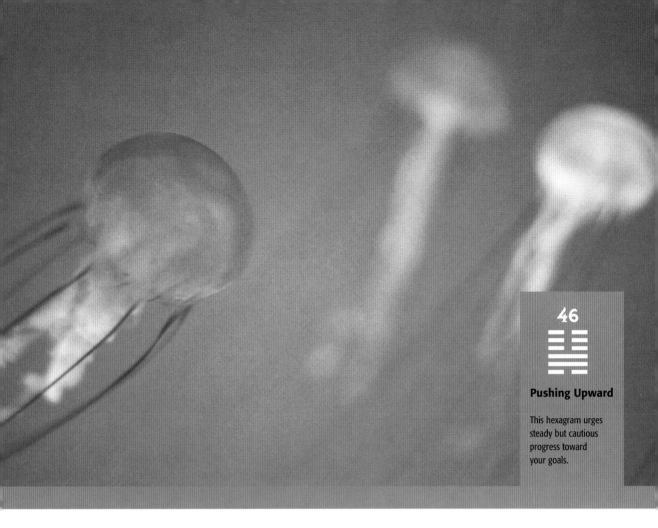

46

Pushing Upward

This hexagram urges steady but cautious progress toward your goals.

47 Oppression

Hardship and adversity. Keep your head and weather the storm. Be determined and strong.

48 The Well

A time of peace and good fortune. Be still and avoid action. Concentrate on development of inner self.

49 Revolution

Rapid change is inevitable. Accept the change, adapt as required, and move forward.

50 The Cauldron

Great good fortune and stability. Cautious conservatism may be rewarded. Check the details.

51 Thunder

Expect the unexpected, good and bad. Keep your spirits up and weather the storm; it will pass.

52 Keeping Still

Withdraw, wait, and watch. Obstructions will pass. This is a time for recuperation.

55

Abundance

This hexagram
indicates that a time
of plenty is arriving,
but warns against
extravagance.

53 Development
Slow progress. Do not expect too much. Avoid hasty actions and learn to exercise patience.

54 The Marrying Maiden
Accept what you have for the moment and be patient. Rash or improper action invites disaster.

55 Abundance
Prosperity, luck, and riches. Enjoy the moment, but beware of extravagance; all things change in time.

56
The Stranger

This hexagram is a warning against overconfidence, and urges caution when choosing your friends.

56 The Stranger
Do not be lulled into overconfidence. All is not as secure as it seems. Choose friends cautiously.

57 Penetrating Wind
Look before you leap. Take the easiest course around obstacles. Slow but sure is your best recourse.

58 Joy
You never had it so good. Enjoy yourself, but maintain vigilance. Share your joy with others.

59 Dispersion
Better times are coming, but this does not mean you can be reckless. Cooperation will bring contentment.

60 Limitation
Restraint is called for. Accept your limitations and you will progress. Follow the rules.

61 Insight
Trust and sincerity will win the support of colleagues. Pretense will invite trouble.

62 Minor Success
This is no time for ambitious projects. Keep within limitations. Look for success in small things.

63 Completion
Completion is achieved. Fame and success. Take care not to lose what has been gained.

64 Near Completion
Almost there. Success is within reach if caution is maintained. Avoid risks and arguments.

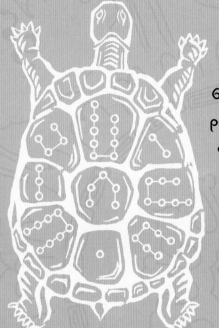

The Chinese magic square, called the lo shu, has been a traditional good luck symbol for up to 6,000 years. Legend says it was discovered in the pattern of markings found on the back of a turtle that appeared on the river Lo during a devastating flood. (The turtle was one of the four celestial animals in ancient China, along with the dragon, phoenix, and tiger.) The pattern suggested the numbers one to nine, and it is these nine numbers in their relative places in the lo shu magic square that form the basis of Chinese magic square astrology.

MAGIC SQUARE ASTROLOGY

THE LO SHU MAGIC SQUARE

South

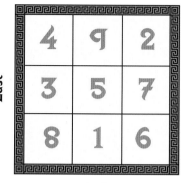

East   West

4	9	2
3	5	7
8	1	6

North

The Lo Shu Magic Square

If you add any line of three numbers in the original lo shu magic square, in any direction, you will find that the result is 15. This is the number of days in each of the 24 phases of the Chinese solar calendar, and was taken as proof of a divine order.

Each number and location has a particular meaning. The number five in the center represents stability and the earth, and the outer numbers correspond with the eight bagua compass points used in feng shui, and with the eight trigrams at the core of the I Ching. North is always shown at the base of the square in accordance with Chinese tradition, south at the top, east to the left, and west to the right.

The number five is at the center of the original lo shu magic square, and represents the stability of the earth.

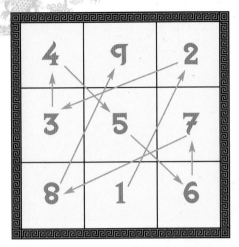

▲ The numbers in the magic square move annually, each number relocating to the section previously occupied by the next largest number in value.

The Annual Cycle

The positions of the numbers in the magic square change annually, with each number in the square moving to the position currently occupied by the next number up. In other words, number one moves to the position currently occupied by number two, number two moves to the position currently occupied by number three, and so on. There are nine possible magic square permutations, each with a different number residing in the central square. Whichever number is in the center of the magic square during a particular year determines the prime influence for that year, and the annual cycle repeats itself every nine years.

► The nine different permutations of the magic square, and the current cycle of nine years with which they are associated. The cycle will continue in this order, with the square for 2001 becoming dominant once more in 2010, and so on.

MAGIC NUMBERS AND THEIR ASSOCIATIONS

Number	Element	Direction	Aspect	Area of Influence	Color
1	Water	North	Yin	Career, work success	Black, navy blue, translucent
2	Earth	Southwest	Yin	Love, marriage	Yellow ocher
3	Wood	East	Yang	Health, family	Green, brown
4	Wood	Southeast	Yin	Wealth, prosperity	Light blue, green
5	Earth	Center	Yin/Yang	Misfortune	Yellow
6	Metal	Northwest	Yang	Friends, communication	Black, white, gray
7	Metal	West	Yin	Children, creativity	White, silver, gold
8	Earth	Northeast	Yang	Education, knowledge	Yellow, blue, black, green
9	Fire	South	Yang	Recognition, fame	Red, purple, orange

2001

7	3	5
6	8	1
2	4	9

2002

6	2	4
5	7	9
1	3	8

2003

5	1	3
4	6	8
9	2	7

2004

4	9	2
3	5	7
8	1	6

2005

3	8	1
2	4	6
7	9	5

2006

2	7	9
1	3	5
6	8	4

2007

1	6	8
9	2	4
5	7	3

2008

9	5	7
8	1	3
4	6	2

2009

8	4	6
7	9	2
3	5	1

Cycles Within Cycles

The annual cycle is itself part of a larger 20-year cycle. A complete cycle comprises 180 years consisting of nine periods, each of 20 years' duration. One particular central magic square number is believed to reign for each 20-year period, even though all the numbers, including the center number, continue to rotate their positions according to the annual nine-year cycle.

The central number dominating the current 20-year cycle is seven, so we are said to be living in the Period of Seven (1984–2003). It is thought lucky to utilize the number of the current period wherever you can in your life, such as by having it in your address or telephone number. The next period will be governed by the magic number eight, but any charts you have made for a house or a birth during the Period of Seven will still hold. The auspices of the Period of Eight will only affect new enterprises.

Finding Your Personal Birth Number

The magic square number that governed the year of your birth is thought to affect your personality and fortune. Look at the chart on the right to discover your birth number, then read about your magic square number personality on pages 45–48. Note that the numbers change each year on February 4 in accordance with the solar calendar, so if your birthday falls before that date, look for the magic number of the previous year.

▲ We are now living in the Period of Seven (1984–2003), so it is lucky to have that number around you, perhaps in your house number or telephone number.

BIRTH NUMBERS

Birth Number	Years								
9	1928	1937	1946	1955	1964	1973	1982	1991	2000
8	1929	1938	1947	1956	1965	1974	1983	1992	2001
7	1930	1939	1948	1957	1966	1975	1984	1993	2002
6	1931	1940	1949	1958	1967	1976	1985	1994	2003
5	1932	1941	1950	1959	1968	1977	1986	1995	2004
4	1933	1942	1951	1960	1969	1978	1987	1996	2005
3	1934	1943	1952	1961	1970	1979	1988	1997	2006
2	1935	1944	1953	1962	1971	1980	1989	1998	2007
1	1936	1945	1954	1963	1972	1981	1990	1999	2008

Magic Square Number Personalities

1 **Positive traits:** Needs discipline and containment, yet adaptable, adventurous, and good in a crisis. Powerful intuition for assessing situations, with the entrepreneurial ability and will to realize goals through sheer effort. A good mixer with many friends, but can also be laidback, content to be alone, and has a tendency to go with the flow. A good number for relationships in general.
Negative traits: Tends to keep deeper feelings hidden. A habitual worrier who finds it difficult to open up to strangers, but if the trouble is taken to make them feel secure, they blossom. Self-doubt can lead to unreliability, as they are easily persuaded by others.

2 **Positive traits:** Modest, dutiful, practical, and thorough. A natural diplomat, sociable, tactful, nurturing, and supportive of others. Gentle and quiet, a provider of harmony and emotional stability. Generally peaceful and happy in relationships.
Negative traits: The shy dreamer. Better at having ideas than realizing them. Idealistic to the point of self-effacement. Prefers to keep in the background and provide bolder types with good ideas from which they benefit.

3 **Positive traits:** The practical go-getter and problem-solver, full of vitality and optimism. Loves innovation, excitement, and challenges. Inspirational company; certainly not the shy and retiring type. Strongly developed aesthetic sense and love of sensual pleasures. A wise and experienced partner.
Negative traits: At times bold and adventurous to the point of recklessness, and forthright to the point of giving offense. However, such outwardly ambitious behavior masks quite a sensitive and easily wounded soul.

Number three personalities are usually lively and optimistic. They love challenges and are gifted problem-solvers.

People with a number four personality are excellent communicators. Their gentle, affectionate nature attracts many friends to them.

4 **Positive traits:** Irrepressible. An excellent innovator and communicator with a good mind. Intuitive, gentle, and sensitive; an attractive, affectionate personality whose moods can change with the wind. Likely to be prosperous and creative.
Negative traits: The scatterbrain. Life can be an emotional rollercoaster ride. Easily swayed, this likeable, impulsive type is open to the manipulation of those who are more focused. This character will bring their lovers roses, but may find truth and fiction hard to distinguish.

5 **Positive traits:** Loves power, status, and command over others. A good organizer and socializer, not afraid to meet challenges head-on. Boldly creative. This individual will forge a materially successful life and appreciates a secure home.
Negative traits: Needs to be center stage and may overwhelm more sensitive types to get there. Can be inconsiderate, insensitive, and destructive. If not paired with someone who is happy to be led, may suffer serially broken relationships.

6 **Positive traits:** Brave, honest, disciplined, and proud; a leader, not a follower. Clear-sighted, independent, well-organized, self-assured, and likely to succeed. Has high ideals and embodies them. Reliable and admirable.
Negative traits: Can be inflexible, overbearing, opinionated, and self-centered. So strong-willed and unapproachable that social life may be a problem.

The brave, self-assured number six personality requires independence, and usually achieves great success in life.

Although number eight characters are slow to form relationships, they are happiest when in a stable, loving home.

7 Positive traits: This is the passionate, material girl or guy. Loves to spend indulgently, but willing to work hard and earn the money. Outwardly competent, shrewd, self-assured, stylish, and resourceful. The natural teacher, actor, author, activist, or politician. A charismatic late developer.

Negative traits: Relaxation alternating with hard work. Pleasure-seeker easily swayed by temptations. Allowed a slack rope, this character will not stick around. Sometimes self-assured to the point of arrogance.

8 Positive traits: Talented, competitive, and determined, with sound intuition. Likely to accumulate wealth by cautious good planning, but not afraid to take risks. Slow to form relationships. Dependable, reliable, and a homemaker, but can also be playful, outgoing, and a quick-thinker who capitalizes on new ideas.

Negative traits: Stubborn traditionalists, some of whom believe they always know best. Extreme self-assurance and difficulty in communicating feelings can lead to social isolation.

9 Positive traits: Quick-witted, warm, intelligent, and enthusiastic one minute, exhausted and withdrawn the next. Changeable emotions and a lively, vivacious disposition makes this character generally popular, though deeper relationships may prove difficult. A good networker. Capable and versatile when motivated, possibly leading to fame and wealth.

Negative traits: Unreliable and impatient. Fickle, vain, and impressionable, this character may find it hard to commit to tasks or to other people.

Magic Square Divination

The precise location of a number in the magic square, and its position relative to others, is the basis for divination using the magic square as a template. As the numbers rotate through their yearly cycle, the magic square number that dominated your year of birth—your personal birth number (see page 44)—is on the move, and is influenced by constantly changing energy patterns as it travels around the square. Knowing how and where these influences are active or passive is extremely useful when making life choices. If you were thinking of buying a new home, for example, you would be well advised to take note of where both your own personal birth number and the number five (the most powerful magic number, from the original lo shu magic square) currently reside. It is believed that you should avoid moving either toward or away from both of these numbers.

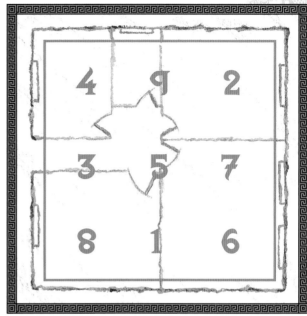

▲ Overlay the annual grid for your birth year onto a ground plan of your home to discover how the energies of the different numbers on your personal magic square relate to the way in which you use your home, then make adjustments accordingly.

You can also overlay the annual grid associated with your birth year on top of a ground plan of your home in order to locate current and future patterns of influence on specific areas, just as you would a bagua compass (see feng shui chapter). However, a simpler way to assess favorable locations for your birth number is to look at the elements that dominate each compass direction, and then assess how they interact with the element that governs your personal number. Those in sympathy will be good locations for you, and vice versa (refer to the cycles of creation and destruction on pages 12–13). For example, if your birth number is one, your governing element is water. Activities in the northwest and west of your home should therefore work well, since they are governed by the element metal, which is beneficial to water. Similarly, southwest may not be very good as it is governed by earth, which is destructive to water.

◄ There are devices and books available that indicate the most favorable compass directions for each magic square number. Alternately, figure them out yourself using the elemental cycles of creation and destruction (see pages 12–13).

FENG SHUI

According to feng shui, we exist in active and mutual relationship with our environment. Feng shui literally means "wind water," and aims to harmonize our environment by marrying the location of our activities to the area where chi energy is most supportive. A perfect site concentrates the focus of chi in one area, without preventing its free flow. Feng shui can be applied to the home, business area, garden, or anywhere humans intervene in nature. There are many schools of feng shui; the methods described here are based on the Compass School.

Origins of Feng Shui

Feng shui was originally employed to find the most favorable location for gravesites. The orientation of tombs was important because ancestors were thought to exert a continuing influence on the living from their new level of existence. The future status of a deceased relative might be ensured with a favorable grave location and appropriate rites. In return it was hoped the deceased would bless living relatives. Bodies were not buried at all until favorable sites had been found, and if later divination suggested a poor site had been chosen, a more advantageous reburial might well take place.

▲ Chinese graves, such as the imperial ones pictured here, are located according to feng shui principles.

A favorable compass direction was essential, but astronomical and geophysical factors were also considered when choosing the gravesite. To face south was regarded as the most propitious direction, and most Chinese would still prefer to live and have their ancestors' graves facing in that direction. (In China, south appears at the uppermost point on a compass rather than polar north, because south is considered the primary direction.) Only later was feng shui used to determine favorable locations for structures intended for the living, as well as for the deceased.

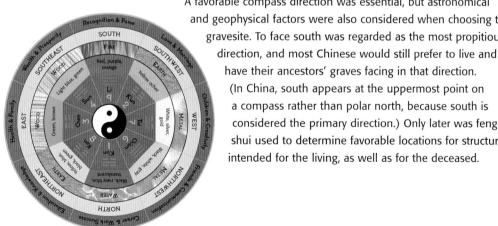

▲ A feng shui bagua, or pa kua, is a compass that shows the ideal locations for particular activities.

Making a Feng Shui Assessment

You can use feng shui to assess your whole home, a room, or even an area in a room such as a desktop. You will need a pencil, a ruler, some tracing paper, and a feng shui bagua compass (see step one).

1. The bagua

The feng shui compass that represents the ideal locations for particular activities is called a bagua or sometimes a pa kua (pa means "eight," kua means "diagram," together translating as "great octagon"). Either use a readymade bagua, or draw or photocopy your own. Your bagua should be inscribed with the eight areas of experience, called enrichments, together with the compass point with which each enrichment is traditionally associated. You may also like to add the magic square numbers, I Ching trigrams, colors, and elements, as shown.

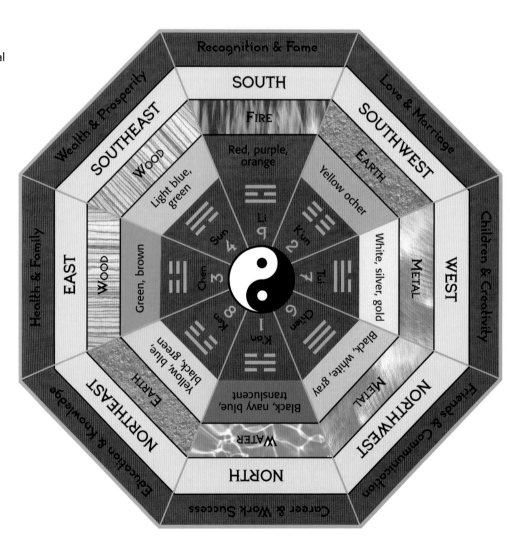

2. Preparing a ground plan

Using tracing paper, sketch a small-scale ground plan for each floor of the property you wish to assess, showing rooms, access ways, doors, and windows, as well as the functions usually carried out in each area—e.g. study, bedroom, kitchen, and so on. Note that it is the function rather than original design plan that counts, so if you use your dining room as a study, make sure that you mark it on the plan as a study and not a dining room.

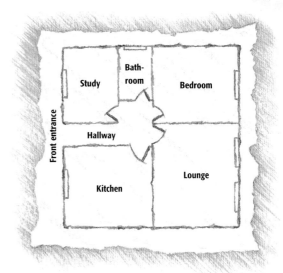

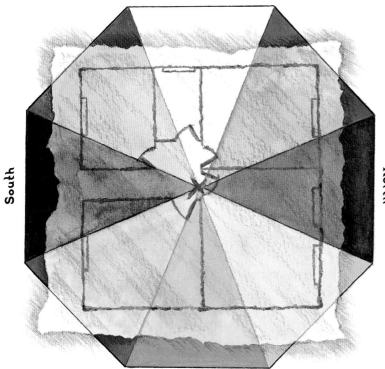

3. Positioning the bagua and ground plan

Overlay the ground plan onto the bagua, so that the center of the plan aligns with the center of the bagua. If your ground plan is a complicated shape, the easiest way to figure out the center is to balance the plan on the flat end of a pencil. When it is balanced, mark the center, then position the plan over the bagua. Next, swivel the bagua until the south section of the bagua is under the site's main entrance, regardless of whether the entrance is really in the south.

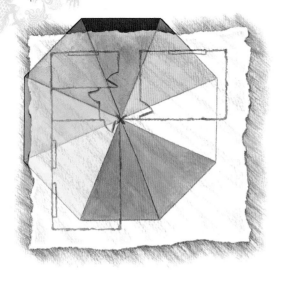

4. Areas of enrichment

The areas of enrichment in regular, square-shaped homes are usually fairly equal in size (as can be seen in step three) and therefore in balance. The areas of enrichment in long and narrow, L-shaped, or irregular-shaped homes are usually unequal in size and therefore out of balance. For example, in an irregular-shaped home, some areas of enrichment may be very small or even missing altogether. Similarly, other areas of enrichment may extend beyond the bagua and therefore indicate an excess of that particular aspect. You can use feng shui remedies (see pages 56–61) to increase missing enrichments and reduce excessive enrichments.

5. Comparing functions and directions

Compare the functions carried out in each area of the property with the ideal functions shown on the bagua. In the example featured in steps two and three, for instance, most of the enrichment for children and creativity falls into the bathroom and only a small portion into the bedroom, which is obviously not ideal. You should also consider the landscape beyond your front door to see if the conditions are favorable or otherwise to healthy chi flowing into your home. If the building's entrance has a poor outlook—for example, a garbage dump opposite—you could have an explanation for experiencing problems. If the entrance has an open aspect, however, then yours may be a very creative and bountiful home. Repeat this comparison for each room in the house, thinking all the while about whether that particular aspect of your life is going well or not, and implementing appropriate feng shui remedies (see pages 56–61) where necessary.

▼ A feng shui consultant visiting a construction site in Vancouver, Canada, to check that the house is favorably aligned.

6. Assessing the flow of chi

The shape of each room and the placement of doors, windows, and furniture will affect how chi flows through your home. The aim is for chi energy to flow steadily and smoothly. Healthy chi flow is encouraged by gentle curves and spaciousness, whereas straight lines and clutter cause chi to speed up or slow down respectively. Chi can also stagnate in recessed corners of a room, and swirl energetically around protruding corners in a disorienting way. Where necessary, use appropriate feng shui remedies (see pages 56–61) to improve the flow of chi.

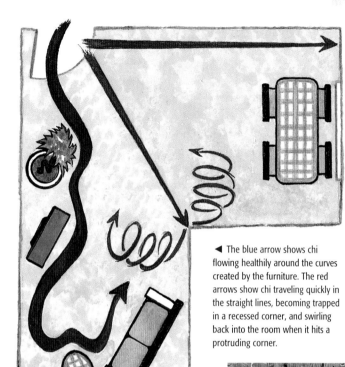

◀ The blue arrow shows chi flowing healthily around the curves created by the furniture. The red arrows show chi traveling quickly in the straight lines, becoming trapped in a recessed corner, and swirling back into the room when it hits a protruding corner.

▲ An imperial dragon on the famous Ming dynasty Nine-dragon Screen in Bei Hai Park, Beijing.

THE CELESTIAL ANIMALS

The Compass School of feng shui associates the four main compass directions with the four celestial animals, each of which is said to govern certain seasons and characteristics.

Direction	Animal	Season	Characteristics
South	Red Phoenix	Summer	Exuberance, brilliance, good fortune, expansiveness, hope
West	White Tiger	Fall	Immediacy, changeability, impulsiveness, strength, violence
North	Black Turtle	Winter	Darkness, mystery, rest, nurture, control
East	Azure Dragon	Spring	Good fortune, wisdom, culture, protection

Feng Shui Remedies

The location of activities within the home is important. Occasionally you may be able to change the function of a room in accordance with the bagua, but this is often not possible and therefore a number of remedies may be needed. For example, you may have your area of marriage and happy relationships located in the bathroom where peace and harmony may quite literally be flushed away. The expedient of keeping the toilet lid down when not in use and the introduction of a neutralizing color are examples of simple remedies for such a predicament. Once the flow of energy is corrected, you should notice a more positive life experience. Positioning your bed so that your head points in the compass direction associated with a particular enrichment is a good way of increasing your luck in that aspect of your life.

Even when the actual function and the idealized bagua function of a room coincides, you may still need to make changes. This could simply mean altering the color scheme to one more harmonious with that function, or rearranging the furniture to allow chi to circulate freely around the room rather than blocking it in one area. In some situations the environment may cause chi energy to flow away from your building or room too quickly, taking with it the positive influences you seek. A strategically placed plant or mobile may act as an entanglement to slow the passage of energy, or make it flow more smoothly.

▲ As well as looking and sounding pretty, wind chimes help to stimulate areas of stagnant chi and entangle and slow down chi that is flowing too fast.

ENTRANCES

The main entrance of your home is extremely important in feng shui. If your front door opens onto an undesirable aspect, such as wasteland or a parking lot, you can minimize any negative influence by placing an octagonal bagua mirror bearing the eight trigrams outside your front door. This will bounce unwanted energy back to its source, but do not use one to rebound your misfortunes onto an unknowing neighbor. The hallway inside the front door should be spacious, bright, and cheerful so that chi can flow easily, rather than narrow or dark. If you have the latter arrangement, make sure your lighting and decorations are bright, and install mirrors to reflect as much available light as possible. Ceilings should be light, as a dark ceiling is like having a storm cloud overhead. Choose wooden furniture or paneling with a vertical grain to avoid financial setbacks coming into your home.

If you discover places in your home where the flow of chi energy is interrupted or runs too swiftly through to benefit you, there are a number of methods you can use to correct faults and maximize beneficial energy. However, some problems are difficult to correct. For example, a house that has a road or path leading directly to the front door will bring trouble straight with it. This sort of mishap is best avoided at the point of purchase, but if this is not possible, such negative aspects can still be mitigated—some well-placed shrubs could be used to soften the impact, for instance.

Mirrors

Use large mirrors to increase the apparent size of a small room in an area where you want more luck and activity. Use convex mirrors to attract more energy; they reflect and bounce the energy around the room so that it stays longer. Use concave mirrors to reduce energy; they absorb it and slow it down. Try to position mirrors so that they reflect a positive image and thereby attract the quality of that image into your home.

Clutter

It is extremely important to avoid clutter, as it entangles chi energy and prevents its healthy flow, resulting in a stagnant environment where nothing can flourish. Spring clean your home regularly and discard any unwanted and unused items to encourage a fresh, healthy flow of chi and a lively, stimulating home.

One of the most important feng shui remedies is to keep the home free from clutter, which can block the flow of chi.

A light, airy environment with lots of reflective surfaces helps to activate chi energy.

Straight Lines and Curves

Long, straight spaces can encourage chi to move too swiftly, so slow it down by placing plants and mirrors at staggered intervals to create a more undulating pathway for the chi to travel along. Break up the straight lines of walls by moving furniture away from the walls and facing it into the room at an angle.

Lights and Crystals

Lights draw energy to them and encourage a good flow of chi. Hang crystals in a window to refract light and bring energy into a room. You can also hang them near a mirror in a dark, stagnant room to activate the chi energy.

Wind Chimes

These stimulate and cleanse the chi energy. Place small wind chimes inside front doors to purify negative influences that enter the home, or situate them in a room where their healing attributes are needed.

Salt and Metal

Place a bowl of salt or a heavy metal object in locations where you wish to stabilize energy, such as in the relationships area.

Plants

Plants can be beneficial everywhere in the home. Use them to soften sharp corners, absorb negative energy, and to change the speed of the flow of chi. Bushy plants with rounded leaves help to slow the flow of chi; plants with pointed leaves are useful for speeding it up. Avoid cut flowers because they no longer contain any life.

▼ Plants help to absorb negative energy and slow the flow of chi.

The curved and heavily planted entrance to this house encourages positive chi to flow steadily into it.

Neutral colors encourage a healthy flow of chi that will help make your home harmonious and welcoming.

Doorways should be kept clear to allow chi to flow through smoothly, and chairs should face the doorway to welcome the chi.

Color

Neutral colors are considered the most harmonious, and help chi to flow smoothly. To encourage success in a particular enrichment, you can introduce that enrichment's color to the appropriate area in your home, perhaps in the form of a painting, wallhanging, vase, or ornament.

Doorways and Windows

Keep doorways clear so that chi can circulate freely, and position seating so that you face the doorway to welcome the chi rather than being "ambushed" by it from behind. Dress windows so that light and chi can enter freely. To prevent chi from leaving a room too quickly, place plants on the windowsill or near the doorway.

The Five Elements

When considering feng shui alignments, it is important to be aware of elemental influences and their cycles of creation and destruction (see pages 12–13). Each area of the bagua is governed by a particular element, which is beneficial to the activity of the area. However, if the functions of the rooms in your home do not coincide with those on the bagua, you could find that you are carrying out certain activities in an area governed by an element that is not conducive to success in that particular activity.

For example, if you and your partner's bedroom is in the northwest instead of the ideal southwest, the dominant metal element of the northwest could consume any earth element that would be beneficial to your relationship. It is therefore important to introduce more of the beneficial element to that area and perhaps to reduce the existing dominant element. So, in this example, you could bring more plants into the room to increase the earth element and introduce a water feature such as a goldfish bowl to reduce the metal element.

▲ A goldfish bowl increases the water element as well as adding beneficial life to the home.

ELEMENTAL STRUCTURES

Certain shapes of building have a dominant element that affects its overall energy. An earth structure's square shape conveys a sense of stability and security. A wooden structure has long, rectangular, or L-shaped lines, and conveys a sense of dependability. A water structure has a rippling, irregular shape, such as the irregular outline of different sections of roof against the sky. This type of structure attracts inconsistency and change. A metal structure exhibits round or crescent shapes in its construction. Such shapes are beneficial for attracting wealth. A fire structure has triangular lines in its construction, and like flickering flames, is conducive to irregular bursts of active and passive energy.

◀ Several elements can be seen in this building's shape. Earth is present in its overall squareness, water is featured in its irregular-shaped roof, but its dominant element is fire due to the many triangular shapes that appear in its construction.

CHANGING Your DESTINY

Your future is not determined by the forecasts you have read, nor the way your life seems to be headed at the moment. This is as true if things are going wonderfully well or if they seem hopeless. No object, person, or state of affairs remains fixed and unchanging. There is nothing you can name or dream of for which this fact is not true.

Embracing Change

The very essence of the Oriental approach to destiny is that it is yours to change. Chinese scholars and sages recognized that everything in nature, without exception, is governed by the laws of change. They observed that the basic energy of the universe, called chi, only becomes known to us as a result of its movement between the polarities of passivity (yin) and action (yang). The symbol used to convey the yin/yang principle shows the swirling of perpetual movement from dark to light and light to dark, each side holding the seed of its opposite already present and about to come into being. This is more than a clever diagram—it mirrors reality.

Developing Strengths and Overcoming Weaknesses

Oracles such as the I Ching divine the direction that change is taking at the moment a question is asked, but the answer given is merely a likely outcome, an indication of what may be, unless you act, or other influences alter that possibility. You always retain your power as a free agent to alter what fate may appear to offer you, and to use the oracles as a means of personal development so that you can develop your strengths and overcome your weaknesses. Always remember that you have control over your own destiny.

- *Know your strengths and weaknesses by reference to your magic square number and the animal and element influencing the moment of your birth. Benefit from these tendencies. Choose the career and relationships that will play to your strengths and avoid those that draw on your weaknesses.*
- *Know when and how to act in specific situations, according to the advice given in the I Ching.*
- *Change the timing of events to an hour or date with more fortunate aspects, using your knowledge of the Chinese calendar.*
- *Alter your environment according to feng shui principles so that the direction of the energy now influencing your life is attracted or deflected as desired.*

▲ A Shang dynasty vase from the 16–15th century B.C. featuring a turtle, one of the four Chinese celestial animals.

Index

Page numbers in *italics*
refer to illustrations

Credits

Quarto would like to thank and acknowledge the following for supplying pictures reproduced in this book:

Key: B = Bottom, T = Top, C = Center, L = Left, R = Right

Ann Ronan Picture Library: Page 21TR. **Art Archive**: Page 4BL, Page CR, Page 9L, Page 15TL, Page 63BL. **Corbis Images**: Page 54BR. **Corel Images**: Pages 4–5, Page 6BL, Page 7B, Page 13TR, Page 15B (background image), Page 16TR, Page 41B, Page 51TR, Page 62BL. **Ian Britton**: Page 44TR. **Images Colour Library**: Page 55BR, Page 7TR, Page 9TL, Page 17BL, Pages 18–19, Page 21BL, Page 28BL, Page 28TR, Page 29TR, Page 30TL, Page 50BL. **Photodisc**: Page 56BR. **Superstock**: Page 14BL.

All other photographs and illustrations are the copyright of Quarto. While every effort has been made to credit contributors, we would like to apologize should there have been any omissions or errors.